TELEMEDICINE

A GATEWAY TO HEALTH CARE

ARYAN CHAUDHARY

This Book is dedicated to “Lord Ram and My Beloved Parents (Navneet and Parul)”

Contents

About The Author

Aryan Chaudhary- Aryan Chaudhary is the Research Head and lead member (the research project launched by Nijji Healthcare Pvt Ltd). He focuses on implementing technologies such as artificial intelligence, deep learning, IoT (Internet of Things), cognitive technology, and the blockchain to better the healthcare sector. He has published academic papers in public health and digital health in international journals and participated as a keynote speaker in many international and national conferences. His research includes the integration of IoT and sensor technology for gathering vital signs through one time/ ambulatory monitoring and then the functionality of Artificial Intelligence, Machine Learning leading to big data analytics for faster intervention, tracking of prognosis and research on these vast data for effective clinical research for future development of treatment, drug, pathological tests and supply systemHe is editor of many books in Biomedical Science and the Chief Editor of CRC Series. He also serves as the guest editor of many special issues in reputed journals. He has been awarded with Most Inspiring Young Leader in Healthtech Space 2022 by Business Connect and the best project leader Global Education and Corporate Leadership . He is the Senior Member of many international association in science

Preface

Telemedicine has existed for decades, as the days pass by, our Technology is evolving and becoming much more engaging. The market is now exploding due to advances in Technology, shortages of medical providers (especially in rural areas), a shift towards population health management and attempts to reduce health care costs. Telemedicine has existed for a period of time. During the period of the Covid-19 pandemic, hospitals and clinics were not an option for mild diseases. At that point in time, Telehealth and Telemedicine became good alternatives. To understand Telemedicine, we need to understand Telehealth. It is the transmission of health-related services and information via digital information and telecommunications technologies, with the goal of providing patient care and improving the entire healthcare delivery system. Telemedicine is a subset of Telehealth defined as the use of telecommunications technologies and providing medical information and services. The effectiveness of Telemedicine depends on increased adoption among providers and patients. Telemedicine has the potential to improve access to health care, particularly in areas where there are geographical barriers, as well as to reduce costs. Telemedicine may take more time to face challenges in connecting virtual communication due to a slow internet connection or a server malfunction. The advancement and integration of information and communication technologies into healthcare delivery hold enormous promise for patients, providers, and payers in future healthcare systems. This Review Book, is an overview of Telemedicine is discussed, which includes applications of Telemedicine, handling and protecting the data, diagnosis process and more things.

Acknowledgements

"Presentation, inspiration and motivation have always played an important role in the success of any venture."

Firstly, I thank the Almighty for his inspiration and benevolence for giving me the opportunity to design the book.

I pay my sincere gratitude to Saikat Mukhopadhyay, who always told me to aim high and says that do not aim low; otherwise, you will miss the mark. I am immensely obligated to my two teachers R.K. Khangar and Akanksha Gupta, for their elevating inspiration, encouraging guidance and kind supervision throughout the journey. I wish to thank the officials at Cambridge Scholar Publishing for their invaluable efforts, great support and valuable advice for this project towards the successful publication of this book

I am deeply grateful to my parents for their support, appreciation, encouragement and keen interest in my academic achievements.

CHAPTER I

Introduction

Telehealth and Telemedicine were described as the electronic exchange of health information among one region and some others to enhance patients' health. Telemedicine is a simple telephone conversation, but increasingly it involves a video call, also known as virtual appointments. It has been proven to be especially useful in underserved communities where there is a shortage or absence of adequate medical care, which includes remote areas. It is also a diverse series of Technology and scientific applications. Telemedicine is a vast term that encompasses any clinical activity concerning the element of distance. It is an assorted assortment of innovations and clinical applications. The introduction of Telemedicine into routine health care is being obstructed by the dearth of scientific proof on its clinical and economic effectiveness. Telemedicine structures may be characterized through the kind of data sent (including radiographs or medical findings) and through the approach used to transmit it. Many regions of scientific exercise have capacity telemedicine applications. Image transmission is a fundamental part of radiology and pathology. Clinically orientated specialties can seize and remotely show bodily findings, transmit specialized facts from exams including electroencephalograms (EEG) and electrocardiograms (ECG), and perform interactive health examinations or interviews. Telemedicine presents numerous advantages that include enhancing access and brief patient engagement at an inexpensive cost; however, moral and legal demanding situations need to be taken under consideration even as implementing telemedicine programs. It holds wonderful capability for lowering the range of diagnoses, in addition, to enhancing the medical management and transport of health care offerings globally through improving access, quality, efficiency, and cost-effectiveness. The great use of ICT (information and communications technology) in medication has opened new horizons to enhance healthcare in India. Telemedicine help doctor-patient encounters withinside the long term because it presents healthcare experts with possibilities for case-based studying that may be implemented in the remedy of future patients. The WHO has said that with reference to its health-for-all method, it recommends that the WHO and its member states must:integrate the appropriate use of health telematics in the overall policy and strategy for the attainment of health for all in the 21st century, thus fulfilling the vision of a world in which the benefits of science, Technology and public health development are made equitably available to all people everywhere."[2]

Telemedicine is the region wherein the medication and facts and telecommunications era meet, is probably the part of this revolution that might have the finest effect on healthcare delivery.

CHAPTER II

Types of Telemedicine

The common thread for all telemedicine applications is that some clients (such as patients or healthcare professionals) receive input from people with extensive experience in the relevant field when the parties are separated in space or time. The types of Telemedicine are classified on the basis of:

- The Client and the expert interaction
- The information transmitted.

The *type of interaction* is usually classified as either store-and-forward or Real-time interaction.

Store-and-Forward Interaction:

Store-and-Forward telemedicine is also known as "asynchronous telemedicine." It is a way through which healthcare providers share patient clinical statistics like lab reports, imaging studies, videos, and different information with a physician, radiologist, or professional at any other location. Store-and-forward Telemedicine saves time and enables practitioners to serve the population through services more fully. Text messages are an example of store-and-forward.

Real-time Interaction:

Interactive services can provide immediate advice to patients with medical needs. During a real-time telemedicine session, patients and healthcare professionals use video conferencing software to hear and see each other. After collecting the medical history and discussing all the symptoms, the providers may be able to do an assessment similar to what is usually done in a face-to-face appointment. Teleneuropsychology is an example of this type of Telemedicine, which includes neuropsychological counselling and telephone assessments for patients with or suspected of having a cognitive impairment.

The *information transmitted* between the two sites can take various forms, including data and text, audio, still images, and video. Classified as Remote patient monitoring and Stored Interactive.

Remote patient monitoring:

Remote patient monitoring, also known as self-monitoring and telemonitoring, relies on patients testing and monitoring themselves at home using various forms of medical technology. The device used by the patient sends the data back to the telemedicine system, where it is received and evaluated by a healthcare professional. Widely used to treat chronic diseases such as cardiovascular disease, diabetes and asthma.

Stored Interactive:

A new type of Telemedicine, Stored Interactive, is considered a storage and delivery technology that is very similar to text messaging but has many of the benefits of interactive services such as live video. Interaction via health chat, for example, allows patients to articulate their symptoms to doctors via recorded video messages. This is more effective than text messages or phone calls for both patients and doctors because it reduces the chance of diagnostic errors while providing convenience not found in online services.

Each type of Telemedicine offers providers a variety of ways to provide efficient and effective patient care. It increases patient access and provides a more convenient way to get the care they need.

CHAPTER III

Categories

Telepharmacy

Because pharmacies are an important structure of the healthcare system and are widely distributed, at least in industrialized countries, they can provide capillary health services. Despite the important role of pharmacies as branches of primary care, the unequal distribution of these structures is striking not only in urban and rural areas but also in developed countries, where distribution at the regional level is scarce. The application of information and communication technologies (ICT) in the healthcare sector can open new perspectives on health care delivery and help address the problem of the declining availability of health care workers. One possibility can be represented by telepharmacy services. Telepharmacy is defined as "the use of communications by registered pharmacists and pharmacies to deliver medicines to patients at remote locations." Already developed telepharmacy services include drug selection, order confirmation and issuance, patient consultation and monitoring, and clinical services. A typical feature of telepharmacy services is that the pharmacist is not physically resident at the pharmacy or patient care location. The benefits of telepharmacy services are represented by the widespread application of pharmaceutical services, even in regions where services are underserved due to economic or geographic issues.

Teleneurology

Teleneurology is a new field in Telemedicine. This can be defined as a neurologist consultation, either remotely or without an in-person visit, using a variety of technologies to provide communication, including phone and internet. Teleneurology, which includes teleconsultation, teleconferencing, and distance education, can be initiated by a physician or patient. The neurologist reported the application of Telemedicine for certain neurological conditions, including headache, dementia, epilepsy, stroke, movement disorders, and multiple sclerosis. The clinical initiative may have been most prominent in accelerated stroke by rapidly assessing a patient's condition before deciding on thrombolytic therapy. The widespread availability of the Internet and the use of search engines, a resource that can influence traditional doctor-patient relationships, are driving the growing use of patient-led teleneurology. Teleneurology will increasingly affect all neurologists.

Teleneuropsychology

The use of videoconferencing technology for diagnosis and treatment in healthcare continues to grow at a rapid pace. Telepsychiatry and its applications have been well received by patients and health care providers, and diagnostic and therapeutic outcomes are broadly similar to traditional face-to-face interactions. Although large-scale studies are lacking, preliminary applications of videoconferencing-based neuropsychological assessments (Teleneuropsychology) have shown promising results with respect to the validity and reliability of several standardized tests. This study was conducted to determine the reliability of a video teleconferencing (VTK) neuropsychological assessment using a short set of standard neuropsychological tests commonly used to assess known or suspected dementia. Tests included the Mini-Mental State Examination (MMSE), Hopkins Verbal Learning Test-Revised, Front and Back Numeric Ranges, Boston Naming Short Test, Letter and Category Fluency, and Clock Drawing. The trial was administered directly to subjects via the VTC, balancing the use of alternative forms of testing and standardized guidelines.

Teletrauma

Teletrauma, also known as "tele-ER" or "tele-emergency care," is a specialized form of Telemedicine that provides remote trauma treatment using telecommunication technologies such as video conferencing. With advances in Technology and the prevalence of high-speed Internet, Teletrauma is becoming increasingly common, especially in remote areas such as rural communities. At times, only 30% of the US population lives within a 60-minute radius of a trauma centre. Teletrauma allows experienced clinicians to monitor patients and communicate remotely with other clinicians. Emergency physicians can use this Technology to evaluate patients and determine if they need to upgrade to a higher level of care. Teletrauma typically incorporates video conferencing tools as well as vital signals transmitted digitally from the patient, including the patient's heart rate, oxygen saturation, heart rate, blood pressure, temperature, and respiration. This information is sent directly to emergency physicians who can monitor patients in real-time and make informed decisions about their condition.

Telerehabilitation

Telerehabilitation (or e-Rehabilitation) - Provision of rehabilitation services through telecommunication networks and the Internet. Most services can be divided into two categories: clinical evaluation (the patient's ability to function in their environment) and clinical care. Some areas of rehabilitation practice in which telerehabilitation has been studied are neuropsychology, speech-language pathology, audiology, occupational therapy, and physical therapy. Telerehabilitation can provide care to people who cannot go to a clinic because of a disability or travel time. Telerehabilitation also allows rehabilitation professionals to engage in clinical counselling remotely.

Two important areas of telerehabilitation research are (1) demonstrating that assessment and treatment are equivalent to personal examination and treatment and (2) creating new data collection systems to digitize information that can be used in practice by therapists. Pioneering research in telehaptics (touch) and virtual reality could expand the scope of telerehabilitation practise in the future.

Telenutrition

Telenutrition refers to the use of videoconferencing/telephone calls for online consultations with a dietitian or nutritionist. Patients or clients upload important statistics, diet logs, food photos, and more to the Telenutrition Portal, which a nutritionist or nutritionist can use to analyze their current health status. A dietitian or dietitian can set goals for clients/ patients and monitor progress on a regular basis with follow-up consultations. The Telenutrition Portal helps clients/patients to get remote advice for themselves and/or their families from the best nutritionists or dietitians around the world. This can be very helpful for elderly/bed-patients who can consult a dietitian without leaving home. Remote feeding has been demonstrated to be possible, and most patients have been scheduled during the COVID-19 pandemic lockdown, but follow-up visits are not provided and have instead relied on nutritional television.

Telecardiology

ECGs or electrocardiograms can be transmitted by phone and wirelessly. ECG inventor Willem Einthoven actually tested ECG transmission over telephone lines. That is because the hospital did not allow him to move patients to his lab outside the hospital to test the new device. In 1906, Einthoven devised a method for transferring data directly from hospitals to laboratories.

One of the oldest known telecardiology systems for remote transmission of ECG was established in 1975. This system provided wireless ECG transmission from a moving ICU van or patient from home to a central station in a medical ward ICU. The radio transmission was performed using frequency modulation to remove noise. Transmission was also carried out over telephone lines. The ECG output was connected to the phone input using a modulator that converts the ECG to a high frequency. At the other end, the demodulator converted the audio to ECG with good amplification accuracy. ECG was converted to sound waves at frequencies ranging from 500 Hz to 2500 Hz with a reference frequency of 1500 Hz.

Teleradiology

Teleradiology is the ability to send radiographic images (X-ray, CT, MRI, PET/CT, SPECT/CT, MG, ultrasound...) from one location to another. The implementation of this process requires three main components: an image transmission station, a transmission network, and a reception image viewing station. The most common implementation is two computers connected via the Internet. The host computer must have a high-quality display screen that has been tested and approved for clinical use. Sometimes the receiving computer has a printer to print images for convenience. The remote radiology process starts at the imaging station. This first step requires a radiographic image and a modem or other connection. The image is scanned and then sent to the receiving computer over a network connection.

Teleradiology is the most popular application of Telemedicine and accounts for at least 50% of all telemedicine usage.

Telepathology

Telepathology is the practice of pathology from a distance. It uses communication technology to facilitate the transfer of rich image pathology data between remote locations for diagnostic, educational, and research purposes. Telepathology requires the pathologist to sample video images for analysis and rendering diagnostics. The precursor to telepathology, the use of "television microscopes," did not require the pathologist to be physically or virtually "manually" involved in selecting the microscope field of view for analysis and diagnosis.

Telepathology has been used successfully in many applications, including visualization of histopathological tissue diagnosis at a distance for educational and research purposes. Digital pathology imaging, including virtual microscopy, is the method of choice for telepathology services in developed countries, but analogue telepathology imaging is still used for patient care in some developing countries.

Telesurgery

Telesurgery (also known as remote surgery) is the ability of a doctor to perform surgery on a patient even if they are not physically in the same location. This is a form of telepresence. Telesurgery combines elements of robotics, high-speed data connections, tactile sensations, and advanced communication technologies such as information management system elements. The field of robotic surgery is quite well established, but most of these robots are controlled by surgeons on the surgical site. Telesurgery is essentially an advanced remote operation for surgeons where the physical distance between the surgeon and the patient is not critical. He promises that the professional surgeon's experience will be provided to patients around the world without the need for patients to travel outside of local hospitals. Telesurgery is the performance of a surgical procedure in which the surgeon is not physically co-located with the patient using a robotic teleoperation system controlled by the surgeon. The remote operator can provide tactile feedback to the user. Telesurgery combines elements of a robot with high-speed data transmission. Although transatlantic surgery has been demonstrated, significant limiting factors are the speed, latency, and reliability of the communication system between the surgeon and the patient.

Telenursing

Telenursing refers to the provision of nursing services using communication and information technology in a medical environment where there is a great physical distance between a patient and a nurse or between several nurses. It is a part of Telehealth and has many points of contact with other medical and non-medical applications such as telediagnosis, teleconsultation, remote monitoring, etc., in rural, small or sparsely populated areas. Among its benefits, telenursing could help address the growing shortage of nurses. Shorten distances, save travel time and keep patients out of hospitals. The job satisfaction of tele-nurses is high.

Telenursing allows patients to communicate with nurses through mobile devices, computers, mobile applications, video technology, and remote patient monitoring. Nurses use a variety of tools when providing care through telenursing. They may send information to patients through an app or website.

CHAPTER IV

Telemedicine vs Telehealth

Telehealth is a subset of E-health, while Telemedicine is a subset of Telehealth. Telehealth provides a broader range of health care services delivered over the Internet than Telemedicine, while Telemedicine provides a limited range of health care services. Telehealth provides both teleclinical and non-clinical services, while Telemedicine only provides teleclinical services over the Internet. Telehealth provides clinical services such as ECG, virtual appointments, remote diagnosis, and prescription filling, as well as non-clinical services such as administrative meetings, provider training and continuing medical training. On the other hand, Telemedicine provides only clinical services such as drug management and expert consultation through safe video recording. Telemedicine is available in general health care services, and Telemedicine covers specific clinical services that provide different types of health care services. Telemedicine refers to the traditional Technology of providing medical diagnosis and screening, while Telehealth can provide various forms of diagnosis, treatment and education. An example of Telemedicine is the exchange of medical data between a health care provider and a patient, and Telehealth includes training medical professionals and general administrative tasks.

Not all Telehealth is Telemedicine. However, all Telemedicine is Telehealth.

Table -Telemedicine vs. Telehealth

Telehealth-

Telehealth is a digital care world.

It is a broad range of Technology.

Its service can be provided by healthcare professionals, including nurses pharmacists.

Telehealth can be useful in medical education

Telemedicine

Telemedicine is the delivery of care via remote experience with a provider.

It is a medical piece of Telehealth.

It is restricted to service delivery by clinical practitioners only.

CHAPTER V

Survey

Whenever distance prevents proper patient care, Telemedicine can be a good solution. The distance can affect care delivery everywhere in terms of time and quality. In both developed and developing countries, situations may arise where the timing of intervention from disease detection to treatment initiation has a significant impact on the outcome of the treatment itself.

The epidemic of 2019 novel coronavirus (severe acute respiratory syndrome coronavirus 2) or COVID-19 has spread from Wuhan to all over China. It has also spread to more and more countries. On March 11, 2020, the WHO declared a global pandemic for the outbreak of the novel coronavirus (COVID-19). Six million people have been confirmed to be infected with COVID-19, and more than 370,000 have died. The emergence of the COVID-19 outbreak has made Telemedicine for both chronic and acute illnesses fast and critically leveraged. The National Health Service (NHS) quickly implemented a telemedicine solution as an alternative to face-to-face counselling during the COVID-19 pandemic. Most health care workers (medical experts) were not familiar with Telemedicine prior to the current pandemic. This soaring prevalence is driven by the need to contain the spread of COVID-19 as many patients use Telemedicine for the first time during the pandemic.

On 9 August 2020, the Government of India introduced eSanjeevani, a telemedicine service, as part of its Digital India initiative. During the COVID-19 pandemic, healthcare workers used video conferencing to diagnose and treat patients in geographically different locations. The platform currently supports two types of telemedicine services. "Doctor-to-Doctor" (eSanjeevani) and "Patient-to-Doctor" (eSanjeevani OPD). These services are part of a larger government plan to connect large hospitals to smaller medical centers in remote areas. As it expands, medical school hospitals and major public hospitals in the States will serve as "hubs" providing teleconsultation services to spokes or primary care centers (hub-and-spoke model).

According to a report by the online portal Practo, the number of online health consultations increased by 500% from March 1 to May 31, 2020.

According to the report, approximately 50 million Indians used online health care during this period, with an average of two online doctor consultations per user per month. During the pandemic, with healthcare professionals offering teleconsultation opportunities, Practo recorded around 80% of new telehealth users, and in-person visits dropped 67%. About 44% of users come from non-metropolitician cities. Of all online consultations, symptoms related to COVID-19 accounted for 7.5%. The average time spent with a doctor online was 8 minutes. A total of total otolaryngology visits was recorded as an increase of 600%, of which 50% were received by people 21-30 years of age. The most discussed issues were ear infections, throat infections, stuffy nose and sinusitis symptoms. About 76% of men and 24% of women consulted online in metropolitan areas such as Chennai, Hyderabad, Delhi, Pune, Mumbai and Bangalore and in non-metropolitan cities such as Indore, Mangalore, Hoshiarpur, Jaipur and Nizamabad.

Tele-counselling related to COVID-19 increased 200% between March and May 2020, with 70% of men and 30% of women coming from urban (70%) and non-metro (30%) cities.

CHAPTER VI

Benefits and drawbacks

Telemedicine encompasses a wide range of care and specialties and includes interactions between patients and providers via phone, email, video chat or conference calls, the Internet, and remote devices. The rapid expansion of Telemedicine coupled with changing regulations and guidelines, particularly during the 2019 coronavirus (COVID19) pandemic, has raised the potential for legal liability and legal challenges.

The original concept of Telemedicine was to provide basic care to rural and disadvantaged patients. The growing acceptance and adoption of Telemedicine can be attributed to several factors. One such factor is the shift in health care services from a fee-for-service model to a model that links reimbursement to patients and quality of outcomes. With increasing pressure and interest on hospitals and service providers to deliver quality patient care and reduce costs, Telemedicine has found acceptance and success in many healthcare specialties and settings.

Telemedicine technology is increasingly being adopted and implemented as an efficient and cost-effective means to provide and access quality health care services and outcomes. Telemedicine has the potential to reduce health care costs in the United States by reducing problems such as substance abuse, unnecessary emergency room visits, and long hospital stays. Telemedicine provides access to resources and patient care in rural areas or areas with a shortage of health care providers, improves efficiencies without increasing net costs, reduces travel and waiting times for patients, and provides equal or improved quality of care. When using Telemedicine, access to care, convenience, and reduced stress can also increase patient satisfaction. Patients and health care providers are enjoying the benefits of Telemedicine, but unfortunately, widespread adoption of Telemedicine is hampered by a variety of barriers, including older adults' use of Technology and Internet bandwidth speeds in rural or underserved areas.

Despite these barriers, telemedicine adoption will continue to grow as patients, and healthcare providers feel more experienced and comfortable with Technology than face-to-face communication. The COVID-19 pandemic has caused many problems throughout the healthcare system. Many changes in care patterns have been required to continue to safely and effectively treat patients with or without COVID-19. This has resulted in a rapid transition to telemedicine models in many settings in inpatient and outpatient. To prevent and reduce the spread of COVID-19, patients and health care providers have had to adapt to the telemedicine model quickly. To prevent the spread of COVID-19, flu, and other infectious diseases, doctors can use Telemedicine to pre-screen patients for possible infectious diseases. Also, there is no need for the patient to come to the office. Less exposure to external microbes benefits everyone, especially those with chronic illnesses, pregnant women, the elderly, or those with compromised immune systems

Disadvantages of Telemedicine include the limitations of comprehensive health checkups, technical difficulties, security breaches, and possible regulatory barriers. Some critics of the use of Telemedicine are concerned that Telemedicine may negatively affect the continuity of care, and because virtual providers do not benefit from a complete medical history and physical examination to aid in diagnosis and treatment, online interactions may be inhumane and claims to be dangerous. Although face-to-face care is required in many cases requiring auscultation or palpation, Telemedicine should be considered as an adjunct and best used in conjunction with face-to-face visits.

Telemedicine also faces many legal and regulatory hurdles, including large gaps in rules, regulations and best practices. This volatility is creating confusion among telehealth providers. Healthcare providers should be aware of risk management strategies and familiarize themselves with the potential legal risks and implications of Telemedicine. This ensures best patient care practices and avoids licensing or litigation issues. Telemedicine rules and regulations vary widely from state to state and are constantly emerging and evolving. This leads to a lack of clear understanding of standards and guidelines among health care institutions and groups. The rapid expansion of Telemedicine and changing regulations and guidelines, especially during the COVID-19 pandemic, increase the likelihood of liability and legal issues. Healthcare providers must be aware of and comply with state and federal laws while using best practices to keep patients safe.

Compared to face-to-face meetings, telemedicine meetings are more vulnerable in terms of privacy and security. Most telemedicine platforms are securely encrypted and comply with the standards and regulations of health insurance portability and accountability laws, but no platform is 100% secure from hackers or data breaches. Another barrier to widespread adoption and adoption of Telemedicine is concerned about the privacy and security of telemedicine systems. Both health care providers and patients must ensure that the transmission of information during telemedicine sessions remains confidential and secure. Several laws protect health information for both face-to-face and telemedicine appointments, including the Health Insurance Transfer and Liability Act, Medical Information Technology for Economic and Clinical Health, and the Children's Online Privacy Act. These laws ensure the privacy, security and protection of health information collected by eligible entities such as health insurance, health information exchanges, and health care providers that use electronic resources to communicate health information. Knowledge of state and federal laws is critical to the practice of Telemedicine. Telemedicine providers should always be held accountable for regulatory compliance, patient privacy, and system security when using the telemedicine model.

In addition to being aware of the legal aspects of Telemedicine, it is important for service providers to know and follow telemedicine etiquette. Healthcare providers must adhere to these standards of etiquette when working remotely from home or performing telemedicine visits in hospitals.

CHAPTER VII

RoadMap

Telemedicine has the potential to be a powerful alternative to traditional acute, chronic and preventive care and can improve clinical outcomes. In industrialized countries, Telemedicine will continue to move health care services from hospitals or clinics to the home. In developing countries or regions with limited infrastructure, Telemedicine is primarily used in applications connecting providers of medical centres, specialty hospitals and tertiary care centres. The future of Telemedicine is based on human factors, economics and Technology.

The future users of Telemedicine will be patients and healthcare providers. However, the patient spectrum will expand to include not only patients but also newly diagnosed, at-risk, "anxious," and health-conscious consumers. Providers will include traditional doctors and nurses but will also include less-skilled health care workers as they are part of the workforce as well as healthcare is adopting a broader team approach. This includes caregivers who may be family members or others.

One of the few advantages of the COVID-19 pandemic is the rise of Telemedicine. Telemedicine expands access to health care for patients who face barriers such as distance (especially in rural areas), transportation, or availability of caregivers. Patients with compromised immunity should no longer be at risk of contracting infectious diseases. Patients who have to wait months to see a specialist in their area can now see a variety of specialists across the country and make an earlier appointment. If a patient accidentally misses an appointment or simply forgets an appointment due to one of these barriers, the provider can continue to provide telemedicine services to the patient, eliminating the need to reschedule, reducing missed opportunities and increasing efficiencies. Most of the limitations of Telemedicine discussed earlier have options and alternatives that make life easier for patients, providers, and institutions. Ultimately, the future of Telemedicine depends on the future of telemedicine cost recovery. Healthcare professionals and patients are getting used to this "new standard" of Telemedicine, but their sustainability depends on reimbursement.

CHAPTER VIII

Conclusion

Telemedicine will complement traditional health care delivery, making high-quality health care accessible to everyone, anywhere one day. Rapid changes in Technology and healthcare make it difficult to predict the role of Telemedicine in future care. Technology trends indicate that over the next few years, healthcare providers will be able to view patients at remote locations using desktop workstations or laptop computers in a mobile wireless configuration. Clinicians can choose between interactive video and save/delivery modes according to their needs. A simple and intuitive software shell provides seamless access to relevant patient records, radiographs, pathology slides, pharmacy information, and billing records. Instant access to an online library of medical information, algorithms for diagnosis and treatment, and educational materials for patients. The government's continued efforts to increase the use of Telemedicine in the face of the COVID-19 pandemic, including eSanjeevani's experience along with private sector initiatives, promise to ease severe healthcare restrictions in India. These telemedicine programs must be widely disseminated even after the pandemic crisis to improve access, equity, education and quality of health care in India. To be successful, you need to prioritize your short-, medium- and long-term goals. In the long run, the Internet infrastructure needs to be improved.

Telemedicine promises to improve access to health care and reduce costs, especially in areas where geographic barriers exist. The field suffers from a glamorous image associated with the use of advanced medical devices and has been criticized for being nothing more than "boys' toys." A technical "solution" to healthcare without understanding the problem. It has been observed that internal NHS networks are a relatively poor means of communication, perhaps for this reason. Patient satisfaction with telephone telemedicine was significantly higher than that of medical staff, including doctors and nurses. Health care providers have reported that they have a good understanding of the purpose and need of Telemedicine during the COVID-19 pandemic. However, the negative attitudes of medical staff towards safety and discomfort had a higher rate of dissatisfaction. The advantage of Telemedicine was the convenience of the patient, and the incomplete patient evaluation was a weakness. In addition, diseases and health conditions that can be monitored using Telemedicine should be clarified through expert discussion and guidance. The adoption of new technologies in healthcare and social work is already a global phenomenon, despite the lack of evidence to support this practice. Undoubtedly, Telemedicine is effective when: specific circumstances. However, the transition to a world where Telemedicine is fully utilized will not happen unless governments and medical institutions develop strategies to encourage progress. Issues to be addressed include ethical and legal issues, resistance to change, lack of infrastructure, language differences and illiteracy, and human and cultural factors such as technological and organizational factors.

Reference

1) https://www.ncbi.nlm.nih.gov/pmc/articles/PMC7577680/

2) World Health Organization. *A HCIIItII Telematics Policy*(document DGO/98.1). Geneva: WHO, 1998

3) https://www.ncbi.nlm.nih.gov/pmc/articles/PMC4410096/

4) Telemedicine in the future, Massachusetts General Hospital, Harvard Medical School, Boston, Massachusetts, USA.

5) Introduction to the practice of Telemedicine, Journal of Telemedicine and Telecare 2005; 11: 3-9

6) Consumer Informatics and Digital Health, Solutions for Health and Health Care

7) Benefits and drawbacks of Telemedicine, Journal of Telemedicine and Telecare Volume 11 Number 2

8) Clinical review-Telemedicine, *BMJ* 2001;323:557–60

9) Telecare, Telehealth and Telemedicine; Science direct, European Geriatric Medicine 1 (2010) 193–197

10) Telemedicine in the future, Journal of Telemedicine and Telecare 2005; 11: 384–390

11) www.practo.com

12) Elford DR. Telemedicine in northern Norway. J Telemed Telecare 1997;3:1–22

13) Hjelm NM, Lee JC, Cheng D, Chui C. Wiring a medical school and teaching hospital for Telemedicine. Int J Med Inform 2002;65:161–6

14) Gulliford SM, Schneider JK, Jorgenson JA. Using telemedicine technology for pharmaceutical services to ambulatory care patients. Am J Health-Syst Pharm 1998;55:1512–15

15) Kristensen GB, Nerhus K, Thue G, Sandberg S. Standardized evaluation of instruments for self-monitoring of blood glucose by patients and a technologist. Clin Chem 2004;50:1068–71

16) Zhang Y, Bai J, Zhou X, et al. First trial of home ECG and blood pressure telemonitoring system in Macau. Telemed J 1997;3:67–72

17) Dyke T, Keake G. The St John Ambulance Service in Port Moresby: a ten-year review, 1984–1993. Papua New Guinea Med J 1996;39:105–10

18) Tonks A, Bennett G. Elder abuse. Br Med J 1999;318:278

19) Mitchell JG, Disney AP. Clinical applications of renal Telemedicine. J Telemed Telecare 1997;3:158–62

20) Pavlopoulos S, Kyriacou E, Berler A, Dembeyiotis S, Koutsouris D. A novel emergency telemedicine system based on wireless communication technology – AMBULANCE. IEEE Trans Inform Technol Biomed 1999;2:261–7

21) WHO. Q&A on coronaviruses (COVID-19). Available from: https://www.who.int/news-room/q-a-detail/q-a-coronaviruses. 2020.

22). van der Hoek L, Pyrc K, Jebbink MF, Vermeulen-Oost W, Berkhout RJ,Wolthers KC, et al. Identification of a new human coronavirus. Nat Med 2004;10(4):368–373. https://doi.org/https://doi.org/10.1038/nm1024.

23) Lipsitch M, Swerdlow DL, Finelli L. Defining the epidemiology of Covid-

19—studies needed. N Engl J Med 2020. https://doi.org/https://doi.org/10.1056/NEJMp2002125.

24) Huang C, Wang Y, Li X, Ren L, Zhao J, Hu Y, et al. Clinical features of patients infected with 2019 novel coronavirus in Wuhan, China The Lancet 2020; 395(10223):497–506. https://doi.org/https://doi.org/10.1016/S0140-6736(20)30183-5.

25) Jiang F, Deng L, Zhang L, Cai Y, Cheung CW, Xia Z. Review of the clinical characteristics of coronavirus disease 2019 (COVID-19). J Gen Intern Med 2020:1–5. https://doi.org/https://doi.org/10.1007/s11606-020-05762-w.

26) WHO Novel coronavirus (2019-nCoV) situation reports. Available from:

https://www.who.int/emergencies/diseases/novel-coronavirus-2019/situation-reports. [Last accessed on 2020 April 2].

27) Smith AC, Thomas E, Snoswell CL, Haydon H, Mehrotra A, Clemensen J, et al. Telehealth for global emergencies: Implications for coronavirus disease 2019 (COVID-19). J Telemed Telecare. 2020:1357633X20916567. https://doi.org/https://doi.org/10.1177/1357633X20916567.

28) Hollander JE, Carr BG. Virtually perfect? Telemedicine for covid-19. N Engl J Med 2020. https://doi.org/https://doi.org/10.1056/NEJMp2003539.

29) Papadimos TJ, Marcolini EG, Hadian M, Hardart GE, Ward N, Levy MM, et al.Ethics of outbreaks position statement. Part 2: family-centered care. Crit Care Med 2018;46(11):1856–1860. https://doi.org/https://doi.org/10.1097/CCM.0000000000003363.

30) Li W, Yang Y, Liu Z-H, Zhao Y-J, Zhang Q, Zhang L, et al. Progression of mental health services during the COVID-19 outbreak in China. Int J Biol Sci 2020;16(10):1732–1738. https://doi.org/ https://doi.org/10.7150/ijbs.45120.

www.ingramcontent.com/pod-product-compliance
Ingram Content Group UK Ltd.
Pitfield, Milton Keynes, MK11 3LW, UK
UKHW022008190726
13853UKWH00004B/1813